KEVIN JOHNSON

THINK

FIGURE OUT WHAT YOU BELIEVE AND WHY

HIGHER
SERIES

 ZONDERVAN®

ZONDERVAN.com/
AUTHORTRACKER
follow your favorite authors

 youth
specialties

YOUTH SPECIALTIES

Think: Figure Out What You Believe and Why
Copyright 2009 by Kevin Johnson

Youth Specialties resources, 300 S. Pierce St., El Cajon, CA 92020 are published by Zondervan, 5300 Patterson Ave. SE, Grand Rapids, MI 49530.

ISBN 978-0-310-28266-2

All Scripture quotations, unless otherwise indicated, are taken from the *Holy Bible, Today's New International Version™*. TNIV®. Copyright 2001, 2005 by International Bible Society. Used by permission of Zondervan. All rights reserved.

Any Internet addresses (websites, blogs, etc.) and telephone numbers printed in this book are offered as a resource. They are not intended in any way to be or imply an endorsement by Youth Specialties, nor does Youth Specialties vouch for the content of these sites and numbers for the life of this book.

Cover design by David Conn
Interior design by SharpSeven Design

Printed in the United States of America

09 10 11 12 13 14 • 20 19 18 17 16 15 14 13 12 11 10 9 8 7 6 5 4 3 2 1

Contents

Start Here

It's time to let your faith fly HIGHER. If you're ready to take your relationship with God to the next level, this series of books shows you how.

Think contains 20 Bible studies that lead you upward. You'll find Scriptures that speak to the core of your life, along with space to express what's on your mind. You'll think for yourself and discover significant insights you might not find on your own. *Think* helps you ponder the big questions of faith. You'll understand that God wants to give you answers—not just about what you believe but why. And you'll figure out for yourself why you don't want to settle for anything less than a faith that makes sense.

Don't rush through *Think*. You can do a study per day, a study per week, or anything between. Actually, the slower you go, the more you'll gain. Each study is just a few pages long but provides you plenty to think about and act on. The end of each study comes with added material to let you fly even higher.

You'll see that every study opens with a mostly-blank page that has a single Bible verse that sums up the main point. These verses are worth memorizing, as a way to fill your head with the amazing truths of God's Word. Then comes **START**, a brief introduction to get you into the topic. **READ** takes you to a Scripture passage. You can read the verses here in the book or, if you want, grab your own Bible and read the passage there. **THINK** helps you examine the main ideas of the text, and **LIVE** makes it easy to apply what you learn. **WRAP** pulls everything together.

Then there's some bonus material. **MORE THOUGHTS TO MULL** tosses you a few more questions to ask yourself or others. **MORE SCRIPTURES TO DIG** leads you to related Bible passages to help you hear even more from God on the topic.

Whether you read on your own or get together with a group, *Think* will help your faith fly high. It's your chance to grab the best that God has in store for you.

Kevin Johnson

1. THE WHOLE TRUTH

Psalm 19:1, 7

The heavens declare the glory of God; the skies proclaim the work of his hands. The law of the Lord is perfect, refreshing the soul. The statutes of the Lord are trustworthy, making wise the simple.

START You might feel close to God when you're looking out from a sun-drenched mountaintop or wandering along a breezy forest path. Enjoying and examining the world truly does teach us indispensible facts about God. Yet there's infinitely more to know. If you want to know all truth about God—and nothing but truth—you'll want to keep looking.

How do you expect to discover life-altering answers about God?

READ Psalm 19:1-4, 7-11

> [1] The heavens declare the glory of God; the skies proclaim the work of his hands.

> [2] Day after day they pour forth speech; night after night they display knowledge.

> [3] They have no speech, they use no words; no sound is heard from them.

> [4] Yet their voice goes out into all the earth, their words to the ends of the world.

> [7] The law of the Lord is perfect, refreshing the soul. The statutes of the Lord are trustworthy, making wise the simple.

> [8] The precepts of the Lord are right, giving joy to the heart. The commands of the Lord are radiant, giving light to the eyes.

> [9] The fear of the Lord is pure, enduring forever. The ordinances of the Lord are sure, and all of them are righteous.

> [10] They are more precious than gold, than much pure gold; they are sweeter than honey, than honey from the honeycomb.

> [11] By them your servant is warned; in keeping them there is great reward.

THINK What exactly can you learn about God by looking around the world? How far does the truth about God spread?

God's glory is his awesome majesty, splendor, perfection, and power.

You can figure out many things about God from the things he's made, his works. You find out even more from the things he says, his words. What do God's words teach you?

The term *law* covers not just dos and don'ts, but everything Scripture reveals about God. The combination of laws, statutes, precepts, commands, and ordinances sums up everything God has disclosed.

This psalm about the works and words of God was penned by King David of the Old Testament. Why does David rely on God's words? What good are they?

LIVE How much do you count on the Bible to discover answers about life? Why is that a good idea—or not?

What facts about God would you miss if you ignored the Bible?

Top of the list: You would overlook everything Jesus shows us about God. Jesus' closest friend, the apostle John, called him "the Word"—God come to earth as a human being to fully reveal who God is. Jesus "became human and made his home among us. He was full of unfailing love and faithfulness. And we have seen his glory, the glory of the Father's one and only Son" (John 1:14, NLT).

How would you explain to your friends how to figure out who God really is?

WRAP The physical universe informs us that a loving and powerful being made the world. But the information we can gather about God just by looking around is incomplete. If we want to discover everything we need to know about the God who made and rules the world, we can't get by without the Bible.

» MORE THOUGHTS TO MULL

- List what you know about God through creation, his works. Then list what you know about God through the Bible, his Word.

- What sources of knowledge do people rely on to supply them with true answers to big questions? How are those sources helpful—or misleading?

- Set a goal of memorizing some of the Bible passages you'll study as you work through this book. You'll find select verses at the start of each chapter.

» MORE SCRIPTURES TO DIG

- Grab a Bible and look at the rest of **Psalm 19**. You've already read most of it. Then flip to **Psalm 119**. It's the longest chapter in the Bible. It happens to be all about the greatness of God's words.

- God's handiwork is so unmistakable that all people know—deep down—that God exists. **Romans 1:19-20** says, "They know the truth about God because he has made it obvious to them. For ever since the world was created, people have seen the earth and sky. Through everything God made, they can clearly see his invisible qualities—his eternal power and divine nature. So they have no excuse for not knowing God" (NLT). God's work of creation shows us enough that we can tell that God put us here, that we belong to him, and that we answer to him. But if we know God only from what we see in the world, our knowledge will be limited. And because all of us are sinful, our understanding of God will be flawed.

- God spoke in words first through his prophets (**2 Peter 1:19-22**) and then through his Son. Jesus is *the* Word (**John 1:1-14**). The Bible wraps together God's words so you can read them firsthand. The Bible tells you how to become friends with God through Jesus and teaches you God's best way to live (**2 Timothy 3:15-16**).

2. THE BOOK

2 Timothy 3:16-17

All Scripture is God-breathed and is useful for teaching, rebuking, correcting and training in righteousness, so that all God's people may be thoroughly equipped for every good work.

START Some who doubt the Bible haven't bothered to find out why it's worth reading or believing. In this next Bible passage the apostle Paul is near death, penning a letter to his young associate Timothy (2 Timothy 4:6-7). He knows Timothy will be a key person to carry on the Christian faith (2 Timothy 1:13-14) and that Timothy's faith will be tested (2 Timothy 1:8-9). Paul offers Timothy three reasons why the Bible's message is worth giving his life to. It's about faces, facts, and feelings.

What do you think about the Bible? Why do you believe it—or not?

READ 2 Timothy 3:10-17

> [10] You, however, know all about my teaching, my way of life, my purpose, faith, patience, love, endurance, [11] persecutions, sufferings— what kinds of things happened to me in Antioch, Iconium and Lystra, the persecutions I endured. Yet the Lord rescued me from all of them. [12] In fact, everyone who wants to live a godly life in Christ Jesus will be persecuted, [13] while evildoers and impostors will go from bad to worse, deceiving and being deceived. [14] But as for you, continue in what you have learned and have become convinced of, because you know those from whom you learned it, [15] and how from infancy you have known the Holy Scriptures, which are able to make you wise for salvation through faith in Christ Jesus. [16] All Scripture is God-breathed and is useful for teaching, rebuking, correcting and training in righteousness, [17] so that all God's people may be thoroughly equipped for every good work.

THINK Paul wants Timothy to remember all that he already knows about Paul and what he's done. Why does Paul say that?

Paul points out that he and others who taught Timothy the faith are worth trusting—and that includes Timothy's mother and grandmother, who are mentioned by name in 2 Timothy 1:5. Like Timothy, you can size up the credibility of Paul, other authors of Scripture, and people in your own life who teach you the Bible. Best yet, you evaluate the trustworthiness of the God revealed in the Bible. Paul studied God and called him "the one in whom I trust" (2 Timothy 1:12, NLT). The first reason to believe the Bible is the credible people who teach you—a reason you can remember as "FACES."

Who is the source of the Bible?

Trusting the people who tell you the Bible is true isn't enough. You want FACTS. The Bible claims to be perfectly inspired by God, "God-breathed." There's solid evidence the Bible is a one-of-a-kind book that could only come from God:

- The Bible presents a consistent message of God saving humankind, even though it contains 66 books written over 1,500 years by some 40 authors.

- The actual words of the Bible are well established. The number, age, and quality of Bible manuscripts far exceed those of any other ancient document.

- The events in the Bible took place in real times and real places— facts verifiable by archaeology.

- Dozens of specific Bible prophecies came true in Christ. Those predictions were spoken hundreds of years before his birth, a sign that the book had origins beyond its human writers.

- The Bible's truthfulness is backed up by the astounding fact of Christ rising from the dead. More on that in study 9.

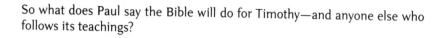

So what does Paul say the Bible will do for Timothy—and anyone else who follows its teachings?

When you test the Bible's teachings in real life, you find that they work. So not only do FACTS and FACES convince you the Bible is true, but FEELINGS will, too. Jesus himself suggests this test: "Anyone who chooses to do the will of God will find out whether my teaching comes from God or whether I speak on my own" (John 7:17).

LIVE Who are the FACES who make the Bible believable for you?

What FACTS about the Bible do you find most persuasive?

How have you been struck by FEELINGS that the Bible rings true—that it works in real life?

WRAP The Bible claims to be true in all times and places, whether or not you believe it. Yet the book itself gives you reasons to trust its message. So, size up the FACES. Think hard about the FACTS. Put the Bible to the test in real life and see if you are persuaded by deep FEELINGS about its truth.

» MORE THOUGHTS TO MULL

- Why does Paul tell Timothy to continue to believe what he has learned and become convinced is true?

- Paul is the author of much of the New Testament. What about Paul leads you to believe his statements about God are true—or not?

- If you doubt the Bible's truthfulness, check with a pastor or another Christian you trust and quiz that person on the Bible's trustworthiness. There's no question you might have that hasn't been asked and answered.

» MORE SCRIPTURES TO DIG

- There's far more to Paul's story than what he tells here. At one point Paul led a drive to kill Christians because he thought it was the right thing to do (**Galatians 1:13**). Later, he suffered and sacrificed much to tell others about Jesus (**2 Corinthians 11:16-33**).

- You don't have to swallow whole what others tell you about the Bible. Dig in and let the Bible answer challenges for itself, like these common objections: "Believing in God is for the weak" (read **2 Corinthians 11:23-27**—that summary of Paul's sufferings). "There are a lot of other good religions. Jesus was just a human teacher" (check **John 14:6**—Jesus claimed to be much more). "Christians are hypocrites— they say one thing and do another" (read **Isaiah 29:13**—God hates hypocrites). "God can't exist because he doesn't answer my prayers" (look at **Psalm 14:1**—God's reality isn't limited to our knowledge or experience of him).

3. SPOKEN WORD

How did the Bible get here?

2 Peter 1:21

For prophecy never had its origin in the human will, but prophets, though human, spoke from God as they were carried along by the Holy Spirit.

START In 2 Timothy 3:16, the apostle Paul said that all Scripture is "God-breathed." He noted that Scripture is good "for teaching, for showing people what is wrong in their lives, for correcting faults, and for teaching how to live right." It ultimately "leads to salvation through faith in Christ Jesus" (2 Timothy 3:15, NCV). But Paul offered no details in that chapter about how God did this inspiring. For that bit of data, look to the apostle Peter, one of Jesus' closest friends.

Where do you think the Bible came from?

READ 2 Peter 1:16-21

[16] For we did not follow cleverly devised stories when we told you about the coming of our Lord Jesus Christ in power, but we were eye-witnesses of his majesty. [17] He received honor and glory from God the Father when the voice came to him from the Majestic Glory, saying, "This is my Son, whom I love; with him I am well pleased." [18] We ourselves heard this voice that came from heaven when we were with him on the sacred mountain.

[19] We also have the prophetic message as something completely reliable, and you will do well to pay attention to it, as to a light shining in a dark place, until the day dawns and the morning star rises in your hearts. [20] Above all, you must understand that no prophecy of Scripture came about by the prophet's own interpretation of things. [21] For prophecy never had its origin in the human will, but prophets, though human, spoke from God as they were carried along by the Holy Spirit.

THINK Peter specifically rules out three possible sources for the God-breathed messages that ultimately became Scripture. Where did these words NOT come from?

If people were not the original source of the Bible, then how did the Bible come to be?

Even though God inspired the Bible, he didn't drop it to earth as a finished product. He spoke Scripture through the unique human personality of each author. Listen to the distinct ways he spoke through just a few Bible writers on the topic of love. Through John: "God is love" (1 John 4:8). Paul: "Follow the way of love" (1 Corinthians 14:1). Jeremiah: "I have loved you with an everlasting love; I have drawn you with unfailing kindness" (Jeremiah 31:3). Hosea: "Plant the good seeds of righteousness, and you will harvest a crop of love" (Hosea 10:12, NLT). Solomon: "A bowl of vegetables with someone you love is better than steak with someone you hate" (Proverbs 15:17, NLT).

What message did the human authors of Scripture want to pass along?

LIVE Why does it matter where the words of the Bible came from?

Say it in your own words: What role did God play in the creation of the Bible?

What did people have to do with the creation of the Bible?

WRAP The Bible claims to come from God. It also makes clear that it came to us via people. If you leave God out of the process, you reduce the Bible to a purely human book. If you lop off people, you make it into a magic manuscript and ignore what the Bible itself demonstrates about its human authors.

» MORE THOUGHTS TO MULL

- Why do people argue about the origin of the Bible?

- How would you explain to someone why both God and people were essential to the writing of the Bible?

- What connection does this passage make between the eyewitness accounts of Jesus from people like Peter and the words spoken by Old Testament prophets?

» MORE SCRIPTURES TO DIG

- Even a quick flip through the Bible shows a wide variety of processes used to write the Bible. Authors reported their interactions with both God and people (**Jonah 3**). They wrote histories of what they had seen, heard, and researched (**Luke 1:1-4**). They recorded their prayers (**Psalm 23**). At times God spoke and told them to take notes (**Revelation 1:11**). They used scribes to put their messages in writing (**Jeremiah 45:1**). All of these methods represent ways Bible authors were "carried along by the Holy Spirit" (**2 Peter 1:21**).

- A little later in life, Peter wrote that Paul's letters were sometimes difficult to understand and easy to distort. Peter and Paul were alive at the same time during the spread of the early church, and they didn't always get along (see **Galatians 2**). But Peter already recognized Paul's writings as Scripture. Check out **2 Peter 3:15-16**.

4. REST ASSURED

Is the Christian faith made up?

John 20:31

But these are written that you may believe that Jesus is the Messiah, the Son of God, and that by believing you may have life in his name.

START In one of the first scenes of the Bible book of John, Jesus applauds a guy named Nathanael for asking tough questions (John 1:47). As the book wraps up, Jesus coaches a disciple whom history has remembered as "doubting Thomas." Don't miss the point of this passage: That it's normal to need convincing about spiritual truth—and the Bible was written so you can believe.

How persuaded are you of the truth of the Christian faith? What convinced you—or what do you still need in order to feel solid in your beliefs?

READ John 20:24-31

24 Now Thomas (also known as Didymus), one of the Twelve, was not with the disciples when Jesus came. 25 So the other disciples told him, "We have seen the Lord!"

But he said to them, "Unless I see the nail marks in his hands and put my finger where the nails were, and put my hand into his side, I will not believe."

26 A week later his disciples were in the house again, and Thomas was with them. Though the doors were locked, Jesus came and stood among them and said, "Peace be with you!" 27 Then he said to Thomas, "Put your finger here; see my hands. Reach out your hand and put it into my side. Stop doubting and believe."

28 Thomas said to him, "My Lord and my God!"

29 Then Jesus told him, "Because you have seen me, you have believed; blessed are those who have not seen and yet have believed."

30 Jesus performed many other signs in the presence of his disciples, which are not recorded in this book. 31 But these are written that you may believe that Jesus is the Messiah, the Son of God, and that by believing you may have life in his name.

THINK It's ten guys against one: What do the other disciples want Thomas to believe?

The phrase "told him" (verse 25) means the disciples repeated and repeated their claim that Jesus was alive. Why doesn't Thomas give in?

The fact that Thomas wants hard evidence is a good sign that Jesus' rising from the dead wasn't a mass hallucination or wishful thinking. Thomas was there. He asked the tough questions you might ask. He got answers.

When Jesus invites Thomas to poke his fingers in the wounds inflicted on the cross, the stunned disciple declines. What does he say instead?

Instead of scolding Thomas for having doubts, Jesus offers the evidence Thomas wants. But Thomas has seen enough. He uses two titles for Jesus, "Lord" and "God"—names only applied to God himself.

LIVE What do you think of John's reason for writing his book about Jesus?

You didn't get a chance to press your fingers into Christ's side or touch the nail wounds in his hands. How can you believe Jesus really lived, died, and rose from the dead if you've never seen him?

WRAP No two people have the exact same spiritual doubts, questions, and hesitations. But God doesn't ban tough debate. He wants you to get facts to ground your faith. Even though you haven't seen Jesus, your conclusion that "Jesus is the Christ, the Son of God" should be based on solid evidence. By believing, you will experience "life in his name."

» MORE THOUGHTS TO MULL

- When is it okay to have spiritual doubts?

- How can skepticism sometimes be unhelpful and less than honest?

- Whom can you count on to help you ask and answer difficult spiritual questions?

» MORE SCRIPTURES TO DIG

- When Jesus appears to his disciples in **John 20:19**, he enters through a locked door. Yet the disciples weren't greeting a ghost. They could touch his hands and side. And in **John 21:13**, Jesus ate. His resurrected body was the same as ours but somehow different. It's like the fresh body that the Bible promises believers will have in heaven (**2 Corinthians 5:1-4**).

- The great Christian teacher Oswald Chambers (1874-1917) said that getting solid spiritual answers is a life-altering experience. He wrote, "Jesus Christ was not a man who twenty centuries ago lived on this earth for thirty-three years and was crucified. He was God Incarnate, manifested at one point of history...The presentation of this fact produces what no other fact in the whole of history could produce: The miracle of God at work in human souls." Read **2 Corinthians 5:14-15** to see how Christ's death and resurrection impacts you right now.

5. SOMETHING FROM NOTHING

Where did the world come from?

Genesis 1:1

In the beginning God created the heavens and the earth.

START You might laugh at the account of the world's beginnings recorded in the first chapters of the Bible. Or you might really dislike Darwin and others asserting that your way-back parents were even hairier than your mother's uncle. Either way, as you read the first chapters of Genesis you can't help but spot a looming claim: There's a designer behind the universe. Your world is no accident.

How do you think the world came to exist? What reasons can you give for your beliefs?

READ Genesis 1:1-4, 26-27, 31

> [1] In the beginning God created the heavens and the earth. [2] Now the earth was formless and empty, darkness was over the surface of the deep, and the Spirit of God was hovering over the waters.
>
> [3] And God said, "Let there be light," and there was light. [4] God saw that the light was good, and he separated the light from the darkness.
>
> [26] Then God said, "Let us make human beings in our image, in our likeness, so that they may rule over the fish in the sea and the birds in the sky, over the livestock and all the wild animals, and over all the creatures that move along the ground."
>
> [27] So God created human beings in his own image, in the image of God he created them; male and female he created them.
>
> [31] God saw all that he had made, and it was very good. And there was evening, and there was morning—the sixth day.

THINK What was the world like before God got his hands on it?

Trick question. God doesn't have hands. Verse 2 points out that the God of the Bible, unlike other gods of the ancient world, is spirit. The Bible also states that God started from scratch. *Formless* and *empty* means there was nothing there, meaning God was the original creator of everything out of nothing, not a repackager of preexisting matter. Again, that's a significant difference from the creation stories of other ancient cultures.

Verses 6-25 show God making the skies and stars as well as plants and animals. At each step of creation, he declares his work is good. After creating human beings, he declares the sum of all he made "very good." Why do you think God is so pleased with his handiwork?

LIVE What do you think motivated God to create?

How does what you know about evolution fit with what you read in the Bible? What matches up—or not?

Do you think it's possible that the world came into existence or that life developed without input from God? Why—or why not?

Agree or disagree—and explain your answer: Genesis was meant for people who lived before modern science, but now we should live by the theory of evolution by micro-mutation and natural selection.

WRAP Understanding how our world originated is immensely important. It's one of the great questions of life. But the most basic questions about the start of the world concern not just "How?" but "Who?" More than anything else, the beginning of the Bible makes a powerful statement about God. He is an all-powerful and all-knowing Being who gave life to us and to everything we see.

» MORE THOUGHTS TO MULL

- What bothers you about the Bible's explanation of the beginning of the world?

- What bugs you about evolution?

- Why does the creation-evolution debate often become so heated?

»   MORE SCRIPTURES TO DIG

- Read **Hebrews 11:3** to see creation-out-of-nothing in the New Testament.

- The Bible has a lot to say about God making human beings. In fact it presents two accounts. The first comes at the end of Genesis 1 (**1:25-2:3**), and the second shows up immediately after that (**Genesis 2:4-25**). The first narrative emphasizes that people are part of creation. The second highlights how God planted people in a beautiful spot and created man and woman for each other.

- If we had the chance to create people, we might make everyone bodybuilders and beauty queens. God, however, designed each of us with a dazzling physical uniqueness that has nothing to do with our culture's values. More than anything else, he cared about our hearts. He equipped us for intense relationships that involve not only our bodies but brains and emotions. And he made us able to be friends with the God of the universe. That's a big part of what the Bible means that we were made in God's "image" (**Genesis 1:27**).

6. RIGHT UP THERE

Is God down on people?

Psalm 8:5-6

You have made them a little lower than the heavenly beings and crowned them with glory and honor. You made them rulers over the works of your hands; you put everything under their feet.

START Some days you might seriously question your worth, as if you're trash even a rat wouldn't drag home to gnaw on. Some people think that's how God views human beings—that when he looks at us, the only thing he sees is a long and ugly smear of sinfulness. This psalm says that view is way off.

In the grand scheme of the universe, how much do you matter? Why do you exist?

READ Psalm 8:1-8

> [1] Lord, our Lord, how majestic is your name in all the earth! You have set your glory above the heavens.
>
> [2] Through the praise of children and infants you have established a stronghold against your enemies, to silence the foe and the avenger.
>
> [3] When I consider your heavens, the work of your fingers, the moon and the stars, which you have set in place, [4] what are mere mortals that you are mindful of them, human beings that you care for them?
>
> [5] You have made them a little lower than the heavenly beings and crowned them with glory and honor.
>
> [6] You made them rulers over the works of your hands; you put everything under their feet: [7] all flocks and herds, and the animals of the wild, [8] the birds in the sky, and the fish in the sea, all that swim the paths of the seas.

THINK This song by King David carefully puts humans in their place—in their spot below God, that is. What reason do people have to honor God? Why call their praise a "stronghold"?

When David ponders the magnificent universe God has made, humans shrink in comparison. That might feel like a crushing putdown of the human species. But what is our real status in the universe?

The Hebrew words for *a little lower than the heavenly beings* could mean either "a little lower than the angels" or even "a little lower than God." Either way, we are nothing short of amazing, made in God's image (Genesis 1:26-27).

What responsibilities does God bequeath to people? Why entrust us with such enormous tasks?

LIVE God thinks people have mind-boggling worth. But that just applies to Christians, right? Agree or disagree—and explain.

Elsewhere in Scripture God spotlights our bad points, like the fact that all people have done wrong and don't measure up to him (Romans 3:23). But even though all people have rebelled against God, including Christ-followers, they retain the great worth God gave them. That's even true of those who still reject him.

How does knowing these facts alter your view of yourself? How does it change your attitude toward God?

One mind-set toward God that is utterly appropriate is gratitude, because everything you are and everything you have are gifts from God. Like Paul asked the people in Corinth: What do you have that you didn't get from God? (1 Corinthians 4:7)

The next time you or someone else gets down on you, how can you remind yourself of your high value?

WRAP You aren't King or Queen of Creation. That kind of supreme title belongs to God alone. But he has shared with you and every other human being an ample portion of his glory.

» MORE THOUGHTS TO MULL

- Make a list of people you've regarded as somehow beneath you. Do something that shows respect for each one.

- Why would God choose to share his glory with people?

- How do you see signs of God's image in the people around you? How do you see that image blemished by sin?

» MORE SCRIPTURES TO DIG

- Part of worshiping God is having a humble awe of God's greatness, respect for his total perfection. It's like a child standing at the feet of a loving, providing parent. In fact Jesus said, "Unless you turn from your sins and become like little children, you will never get into the Kingdom of Heaven. So anyone who becomes as humble as this little child is the greatest in the Kingdom of Heaven" (**Matthew 18:3-4,** NLT).

- Look at **Psalm 139:13-16**, which details how God made you awesome.

- The next time you feel like trash-talking someone, pause and recall that God made that person, like you, "a little lower than the heavenly beings," glistening with his "glory and honor." You can't put down people while you claim to exalt God. The apostle John wrote, "If we say we love God yet hate a brother or sister, we are liars. For if we do not love a fellow believer, whom we have seen, we cannot love God, whom we have not seen" (**1 John 4:20**).

7. THE ONE AND ONLY

Who is Jesus?

Colossians 1:15

The Son is the image of the invisible
God, the firstborn over all creation.

START Back in the ancient city of Colossae, enemies of Christianity tried to shrink Jesus. They said he was—at most—one of many spirit beings who bridged the gap between people and God. The apostle Paul replied to those charges with a soaring explanation of who Jesus is and what he does for us. He's not a guy who can be shrunk to fit our small expectations.

If a friend asked you to describe and define Jesus using ten words or less, what would you say?

READ Colossians 1:15-20

> [15] The Son is the image of the invisible God, the firstborn over all creation. [16] For in him all things were created: things in heaven and on earth, visible and invisible, whether thrones or powers or rulers or authorities; all things have been created through him and for him. [17] He is before all things, and in him all things hold together. [18] And he is the head of the body, the church; he is the beginning and the firstborn from among the dead, so that in everything he might have the supremacy. [19] For God was pleased to have all his fullness dwell in him, [20] and through him to reconcile to himself all things, whether things on earth or things in heaven, by making peace through his blood, shed on the cross.

THINK This dense passage says loads about the greatness of Jesus. So start with this: Who is Jesus?

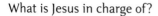

Image means both "likeness" and "manifestation," so Jesus both shows us God and is himself God. *Firstborn* means "first in order" and "first in rank," so Jesus existed before the world and is over the world. John 1:1 wraps together the same ideas: "In the beginning the Word already existed. The Word was with God, and the Word was God" (NLT).

What is Jesus in charge of?

How was Jesus part of the beginning of the world?

Surprising fact: Jesus was involved in creation. Together with the Holy Spirit, God the Father and God the Son form a union so tight it can only be called a *trinity* or *tri-unity*. That teaching runs from the front to the back of the Bible. As one member of the trinity, Jesus was indispensable to crafting the universe.

What did Jesus' death on the cross do for the world?

LIVE After studying Paul's words to the Colossians, what would you add or change in your description of Jesus?

How does the Bible's portrait of Jesus compare to what people around you think of him?

What difference does it make if Jesus is more than an ordinary human being?

WRAP Jesus is no regular guy. He's God in human flesh and Savior of the world. However hard you try, you can't shrink him to human size.

» MORE THOUGHTS TO MULL

- How could you explain Jesus' true identity to a friend who thinks Jesus is something less than God?

- What else do you know about Jesus that shows you he is more than a mere human being?

- Why does it matter that Jesus is truly God?

» MORE SCRIPTURES TO DIG

- Don't miss what Paul says right before this passage. He tells his readers God has made them members of Christ's kingdom of light (**Colossians 1:12-13**). That's the "kingdom of the Son he loves," the complete opposite of Satan's "dominion of darkness," a worldwide reign that's as sinister as it sounds.

- Keep reading in **Colossians 1** to learn more about what Jesus did on the cross. Paul offers this tight statement of how Jesus makes us friends with God: "Once you were alienated from God and were enemies in your minds because of your evil behavior. But now he has reconciled you by Christ's physical body through death to present you holy in his sight, without blemish and free from accusation—if you continue in your faith, established and firm, and do not move from the hope held out in the gospel. This is the gospel that you heard and that has been proclaimed to every creature under heaven, and of which I, Paul, have become a servant." (**Colossians 1:21-23**, NCV).

8. UP FROM THE GRAVE

Did Jesus actually rise from the dead?

1 Corinthians 15:3-4

For what I received I passed on to you as of first importance: that Christ died for our sins according to the Scriptures, that he was buried, that he was raised on the third day according to the Scriptures.

START If you were Jesus and you were trying to prove that you're God—come to earth, in the flesh—rising from the dead tops any list of impressive evidence. After his death was confirmed by a spear thrust into his side (John 19:34), Jesus was laid in the tomb of a wealthy secret follower (John 19:38) and sealed inside with an enormous stone (Matthew 27:60). A crowd of guards kept watch over the grave (Matthew 28:11-15). But Scripture asserts that Jesus didn't stay dead.

Does it matter to you whether Jesus actually rose from the dead? Why—or why not?

READ 1 Corinthians 15:1-8

¹ Now, brothers and sisters, I want to remind you of the gospel I preached to you, which you received and on which you have taken your stand. ² By this gospel you are saved, if you hold firmly to the word I preached to you. Otherwise, you have believed in vain.

³ For what I received I passed on to you as of first importance: that Christ died for our sins according to the Scriptures, ⁴ that he was buried, that he was raised on the third day according to the Scriptures, ⁵ and that he appeared to Cephas, and then to the Twelve. ⁶ After that, he appeared to more than five hundred of the brothers and sisters at the same time, most of whom are still living, though some have fallen asleep. ⁷ Then he appeared to James, then to all the apostles, ⁸ and last of all he appeared to me also, as to one abnormally born.

THINK The apostle Paul says he wants to remind his readers of the gospel—the good news he's shared with them. What are the key points of this amazing good news?

Why is it crucial that Paul's readers hang tight to the facts of this gospel?

Jot a list of the post-resurrection appearances of Jesus noted in this passage. Circle the one that surprises or impresses you most—and explain why.

Paul is making the point that far more than a handful of close disciples saw the Savior. It was a major crowd of people, many of whom could still be called on as star witnesses to the resurrection.

LIVE How persuaded are you by the claim that Jesus was seen alive on multiple occasions after he suffered crucifixion on the cross? Why are those assertions reliable—or not?

Do you believe Jesus literally rose from the dead—that he was truly dead and physically came back to life? Why—or why not?

How does Jesus' rising from the dead demonstrate that he is God in the flesh and Savior of the world?

How would you respond to someone who argues that dead people always stay dead, so Jesus' resurrection automatically has to be a hoax?

WRAP The resurrection of Jesus was a real, physical miracle. It also has a deep, spiritual meaning. Through his resurrection from the dead, Jesus was "appointed the Son of God in power" (Romans 1:4).

》   MORE THOUGHTS TO MULL

- Do you think the early disciples found it easy to believe Jesus had risen? Why—or why not?

- What objections have you heard to our Christian belief that Jesus came back from the dead? How do you answer those?

- If you worry that accounts of the resurrection are borrowed from other ancient religions, grab a copy of *The Case for the Real Jesus* by Lee Strobel and look at Challenge 4: "Christianity's Beliefs about Jesus Were Copied from Pagan Religions."

》   MORE SCRIPTURES TO DIG

- As you check out the Bible's accounts of Jesus' resurrection, recall these words from the apostle Peter: "For we did not follow cleverly devised stories when we told you about the coming of our Lord Jesus Christ in power, but we were eyewitnesses of his majesty" (**2 Peter 1:16**).

- You can read about Jesus' resurrection appearances for yourself: Jesus first appeared at the empty tomb (**John 20:11-18**). That same day he appeared to two travelers (**Luke 24:13-32**), to Peter in Jerusalem (**Luke 24:34**), and to ten of the disciples—all but Thomas (**John 20:19-25**). A week later he showed up for all of the disciples, including Thomas, who had doubted that Jesus was really alive (**John 20:26-31**). Before Jesus headed to heaven 40 days later (**Luke 24:50-53**), he appeared to seven (**John 21:1-23**) and eleven of his disciples (**Matthew 28:16-20**), to James (**1 Corinthians 15:7**), and to more than 500 of his followers (**1 Corinthians 15:6**).

- Fierce persecution scattered Jesus' followers not long after the resurrection accounts (**Acts 8:1-3**). The truth of the resurrection explains why the same disciples who hid after the cross (**John 20:19**) were suddenly willing to be tortured and killed for Jesus. People rarely are willing to die for something they know to be a lie.

9. REALLY ALIVE

Why does it matter that Jesus rose again?

1 Corinthians 15:17

And if Christ has not been raised, your faith is futile.

START Back in Bible times, no one claimed there was still a body in the tomb where Jesus had been laid. Everyone—from the disciples to hostile religious authorities—wondered where Jesus went. And the allegation that the disciples stole and stashed the body of Jesus requires that the frightened disciples went knowingly to their deaths to protect a failed messiah. The best explanation of the empty tomb is that Jesus rose from the dead just as he promised (Matthew 16:21). His resurrection isn't an optional accessory for your faith, like fuzzy dice to a car. Getting rid of the resurrection is like removing the engine.

Suppose some archaeologists dug up a body in the Middle East and proved beyond any doubt that it was Jesus. What would that do to your faith? Does it matter if Jesus really rose from the dead? Why—or why not?

READ 1 Corinthians 15:12-19

[12] But if it is preached that Christ has been raised from the dead, how can some of you say that there is no resurrection of the dead? [13] If there is no resurrection of the dead, then not even Christ has been raised. [14] And if Christ has not been raised, our preaching is useless and so is your faith. [15] More than that, we are then found to be false witnesses about God, for we have testified about God that he raised Christ from the dead. But he did not raise him if in fact the dead are not raised. [16] For if the dead are not raised, then Christ has not been raised either. [17] And if Christ has not been raised, your faith is futile; you are still in your sins. [18] Then those also who have fallen asleep in Christ are lost. [19] If only for this life we have hope in Christ, we are to be pitied more than all others.

THINK Catch the first point: What does the resurrection of Jesus have to do with our own rising from the dead?

If Jesus didn't really spring from the grave, what consequences would we face? Spot at least three problems we'd have to deal with.

If Jesus isn't alive, why should believers be pitied "more than all others"?

LIVE Do you think Christians need to ponder heady questions like the reality and meaning of the resurrection—or should we just get on with our relationship with Jesus? Explain.

Paul claims Christ's resurrection is an indispensable truth. Why does the resurrection matter to you—or not?

First Corinthians 6:14 says the same power that raised Christ will someday raise you from the grave. And that same resurrection power strengthens you today to follow Jesus. Paul wrote, "I also pray that you will understand the incredible greatness of God's power for us who believe him. This is the same mighty power that raised Christ from the dead and seated him in the place of honor at God's right hand in the heavenly realms" (Ephesians 1:19-20, NLT).

What good is your faith if the resurrection is a lie?

WRAP The Bible unashamedly admits that if Jesus didn't rise up from the dead, Christians need a gigantic pity party. Why? If Jesus didn't come back from the dead, then 1) Nothing has put us right with God. 2) We have no reason to think we will rise to eternal life. And 3) Our faith is built on a fraud. The resurrection isn't just an abstract belief for Bible scholars to bat around. It matters to you—right here, right now.

»   MORE THOUGHTS TO MULL

- How eager are you to think hard about the facts of your faith—or not?

- Along with the resurrection what other beliefs are essential to authentic Christian faith?

- Tell someone about the hope you have because Jesus really rose from the dead.

»   MORE SCRIPTURES TO DIG

- Once when Paul was in the city of Athens preaching "the good news about Jesus and the resurrection," a crowd of Stoic and Epicurean philosophers debated the merits of his arguments. Some called him a babbler, others an advocate of foreign gods. They ushered him to the Areopagus so they could hear more about his "strange ideas" (**Acts 17:16-21**). Read their reaction to his preaching in **Acts 17:22-34**.

- Paul caused "a great uproar" by his stand for the resurrection. Troops had to rescue him from being torn in pieces by two opposing sides. Check it out in **Acts 23:6-10**.

- Read **Acts 26**, where Paul explains the reality of Christ's resurrection to a Roman ruler. When a court officer accuses Paul of insanity, the apostle appeals to the king by pointing out that the facts of the resurrection could be easily verified: "Paul said, 'Most excellent Festus, I am not crazy. My words are true and sensible. King Agrippa knows about these things, and I can speak freely to him. I know he has heard about all of these things, because they did not happen off in a corner'" (**Acts 26:25**, NCV).

10. GOOD TO GO?

Does being good get you into heaven?

Romans 3:23-24

For all have sinned and fall short of the glory of God, and all are justified freely by his grace through the redemption that came by Christ Jesus.

START If God were a Santa Claus who kept naughty-and-nice lists, you might guess which list we'd all wind up on. Actually, "naughty" is far too tame a description for how humans act. Romans 3:11-12 says, "There is no one who understands. There is no one who seeks God. All have turned away, they have become worthless; there is no one who does good, not even one." At every turn we fail to keep God's law, his rules for living and relating to him.

So if no one is good, what makes us acceptable to God?

READ Romans 3:20-26

[20] Therefore no one will be declared righteous in God's sight by observing the law; rather, through the law we become conscious of our sin. [21] But now apart from the law the righteousness of God has been made known, to which the Law and the Prophets testify. [22] This righteousness is given through faith in Jesus Christ to all who believe. There is no difference between Jew and Gentile, [23] for all have sinned and fall short of the glory of God, [24] and all are justified freely by his grace through the redemption that came by Christ Jesus. [25] God presented Christ as a sacrifice of atonement, through the shedding of his blood—to be received by faith. He did this to demonstrate his justice, because in his forbearance he had left the sins committed beforehand unpunished—[26]he did it to demonstrate his justice at the present time, so as to be just and the one who justifies those who have faith in Jesus.

THINK All human beings are "under the law," that is, subject to God's rules. What do those rules do for us? What can't they do?

Rules can't make you look good before God. The apostle Paul goes on to say we can't get right with God by acting good (Romans 3:28). Being a good person—even loving others and wildly devoting ourselves to the teachings of our faith—isn't what makes us acceptable to God.

So what does God do to solve our problem?

This passage sums up one of the Bible's biggest concepts. *Justification* means God declaring you not guilty. You are made acceptable to God by grace, his free gift, through faith, trusting in his death on your behalf. You're "justified by grace through faith."

Who can take advantage of God's offer to get right with him?

LIVE Is God impressed when we do good? Explain.

If being good doesn't score points with God, why bother to behave?

Say it in your words: How do you get right with God?

WRAP As good as some people look on the outside, it's impossible for any of us to measure up to God's perfection. Compared to God, we all fall short. A real relationship with God happens through Jesus.

» MORE THOUGHTS TO MULL

- Make a list of all the things you've done that you think impress God. Then tear it up and say thanks to God for sending Jesus to make you right with him.

- If you have never told God that you trust Christ's death on your behalf, tell him now—and tell a mature Christian, too.

- Does this seem to you like a fair way for God to deal with sin? How come?

» MORE SCRIPTURES TO DIG

- Grab a peek at what God gives you when you get right with God: He declares you not guilty of sin (**Romans 3:24**). You get peace with him (**Romans 5:1**). You have been adopted by a loving parent who will never abandon you (**Galatians 3:26**). And you can boldly run into God's presence (**Hebrews 10:19-22**).

- Check out **Galatians 1:1-10** to see the importance of how we get right with God. If you want to dig in deep, look at how Paul chews out people trying to get right with God by good deeds (**Galatians 3:1-25**).

- This Bible passage lays out the facts of what God has done for us. Other Bible chunks emphasize our right response to these facts. We have all done wrong against God. We've all wrecked our relationship with him to the point that we have earned eternal separation from him. We are, however, made right with God when we accept those facts. In some spots the Bible calls that having faith (like here in **Romans 3:22-24**). In **Titus 3:8** it's called trusting God.

11. KNOWING GOD

How can I have a relationship with God?

John 3:16

For God so loved the world that he gave his one and only Son, that whoever believes in him shall not perish but have eternal life.

START One night, back in Bible times, a religious leader named Nicodemus snuck through the darkness to visit Jesus. Nicodemus knew that only God's power could explain the miracles Jesus had done. But Jesus tells Nicodemus a real relationship with God starts only when a person is spiritually reborn. While Nicodemus puzzles over that one, Jesus explains that he is the way to that fresh relationship with God. He utters the Bible's most famous words— John 3:16. Then he speaks some other words you've maybe never heard.

What does it take to get to know God?

READ John 3:16-21

[16] For God so loved the world that he gave his one and only Son, that whoever believes in him shall not perish but have eternal life. [17] For God did not send his Son into the world to condemn the world, but to save the world through him. [18] Whoever believes in him is not condemned but whoever does not believe stands condemned already because they have not believed in the name of God's one and only Son. [19] This is the verdict: Light has come into the world, but people loved darkness instead of light because their deeds were evil. [20] All those who do evil hate the light, and will not come into the light for fear that their deeds will be exposed. [21] But those who live by the truth come into the light, so that it may be seen plainly that what they have done has been done in the sight of God.

THINK So why did God send his Son to the world?

If we believe Jesus is who he claims to be, what does God do for us?

Contrary to popular opinion, God didn't send Jesus to spy on the human race and remind us how rotten we are. What did Jesus really come to do?

Why do people reject Jesus?

There's no difference in the guilt of Christians and non-Christians. All people have done evil, sinning against God and others. The difference between Christians and non-Christians is their acceptance of what God has done for them. While unbelievers hide from God, believers get close to him so they can be healed. Not only do Christians admit they've done wrong, but they also accept that God sent his Son as the sacrifice for the sins.

LIVE Get personal: Do you believe in Jesus the way this passage describes? Explain.

What does this passage say about people who don't believe? Do you agree with that?

This Bible chunk promises that God saves people who believe in Jesus, giving them the gift of eternal life with him in heaven. How would you explain that to a friend?

WRAP Believing in God isn't just jamming facts in your head. It's putting your trust in all of who Jesus is—who he is, what he teaches, and everything he accomplished for you through his life, death, and resurrection. Real religion isn't a game focused on batting around big spiritual ideas or tying each other up with rules. Jesus wanted Nicodemus to know that he was offering way more than that. Jesus came to earth so you could know that God wants to have a relationship with you and the rest of the world he made.

» MORE THOUGHTS TO MULL

- Does it bother you that entering into a relationship with God seems so simple? Why—or why not?

- Do you think God is needy because he wants to be friends with human beings? Explain.

- Have you ever spoken or acted in a condemning way toward someone who doesn't trust in Jesus? Is there anything you can do to fix that relationship now?

» MORE SCRIPTURES TO DIG

- Check out Jesus' whole exchange with Nicodemus in **John 3:1-21.** It's where Jesus says we need to be born again or born from above. Nicodemus misses the spiritual meaning of that phrase. He scratches his head and wonders how a baby can squeeze back into its mother's womb.

- Belief or faith in and of itself isn't what saves you. Believing is humbly receiving what God has already done for you. **Ephesians 2:8-9** explains that nothing you can do is good enough to save yourself: "God saved you by his grace when you believed. And you can't take credit for this; it is a gift from God. Salvation is not a reward for the good things we have done, so none of us can boast about it" (NLT). Grace is God's unearned favor that gives us a relationship with God as a total gift.

12. SO WRONG

How can God exist when the world is so evil?

Romans 5:17 (NLT)

For the sin of this one man, Adam, caused death to rule over many. But even greater is God's wonderful grace and his gift of righteousness, for all who receive it will live in triumph over sin and death through this one man, Jesus Christ.

START Don't be shocked when people blame God for evil. After all, the reasoning goes, if God is all-powerful then he must not be very kind—or he would step in and put a halt to evil. If he's totally kind, then he must not be too powerful—because no truly powerful God would stand by while evil rampages. But before we blame God, we need to figure out where evil comes from.

What's up with God when bad things happen? How is he responsible for evil—or not?

READ Romans 5:12-20 (NLT)

> [12] When Adam sinned, sin entered the world. Adam's sin brought death, so death spread to everyone, for everyone sinned. [13] Yes, people sinned even before the law was given. But it was not counted as sin because there was not yet any law to break. [14] Still, everyone died—from the time of Adam to the time of Moses—even those who did not disobey an explicit commandment of God, as Adam did. Now Adam is a symbol, a representation of Christ, who was yet to come. [15] But there is a great difference between Adam's sin and God's gracious gift. For the sin of this one man, Adam, brought death to many. But even greater is God's wonderful grace and his gift of forgiveness to many through this other man, Jesus Christ. [16] And the result of God's gracious gift is very different from the result of that one man's sin. For Adam's sin led to condemnation, but God's free gift leads to our being made right with God, even though we are guilty of many sins. [17] For the sin of this one man, Adam, caused death to rule over many. But even greater is God's wonderful grace and his gift of righteousness, for all who receive it will live in triumph over sin and death through this one man, Jesus Christ.

[18]Yes, Adam's one sin brings condemnation for everyone, but Christ's one act of righteousness brings a right relationship with God and new life for everyone. [19] Because one person disobeyed God, many people became sinners. But because one other person obeyed God, many will be made righteous. [20] God's law was given so that all people could see how sinful they were. But as people sinned more and more, God's wonderful grace became more abundant.

THINK Genesis 3 tells the story of Adam and Eve eating fruit God had said was out of bounds. What did their disobedient actions way back in the Garden of Eden bring to the entire world?

The Bible argues that death spread to everyone because everyone sinned. Sometimes our sin brings destruction on ourselves, like if we drive drunk and plow our car into a tree. At other times innocent people suffer because of other people's sins, like when a child is abused. And sin impacts not just people but all of creation, so that even the natural world is somehow broken. Romans 8:20 says sin undid the harmony God intended for our world. Romans 8:21 says, "The creation looks forward to the day when it will join God's children in glorious freedom from death and decay" (NLT).

If Adam infected the human race with the nasty disease of death, what good thing did Jesus do?

LIVE So who is responsible for the world's evil? Why?

The Bible says Adam was responsible for the start of evil. Even if that's hard for you or your non-Christian friends to swallow, you still have to reckon with this: Each one of us is undeniably responsible for its spread.

Even if you accept that people are to blame for the world's trouble, then why doesn't God step in and stop evil?

The fact is: God did step in and stop evil. Even when human beings hated God, he sent Jesus to win forgiveness and new life for us—a far better alternative than taking away our freedom to choose or snuffing us out altogether. At the cross Jesus struck a fatal blow to Satan and the forces of evil (Colossians 2:14-15), but it's up to each of us to choose to participate in his plan.

Do you buy this theodicy, this explanation of the relationship between God and evil? Why—or why not?

WRAP Many people who blame God for the world's evils seem to be far less concerned about acknowledging their own guilt and fixing their own behavior than they are about blaming God. He's the one who came up with a practical plan to end evil on a cosmic scale.

» MORE THOUGHTS TO MULL

- What are you going to do today to stop sin in your own life?

- Why doesn't God punish people as soon as they do wrong?

- What is the cause of big bad things in the world, like cancer or natural disasters?

» MORE SCRIPTURES TO DIG

- Have a look at **Galatians 6:7-9**, which promises that you reap what you sow.

- We might want God to rapidly punish every evil deed. While God has promised to squash evil, his plan is built on patience: "The Lord is not slow in doing what he promised—the way some people understand slowness. But God is being patient with you. He does not want anyone to be lost, but he wants all people to change their hearts and lives" (**2 Peter 3:9**, NCV). God gives us time to come back to him and his ways.

- God's patience with human beings means that we often suffer wrong, even when we try really hard to do right. Check **James 1:2-8** for encouragement when evil leaves you bruised and beaten.

13. STILL STRONG

Are Christians weak?

2 Corinthians 11:25

Three times I was beaten with rods, once I was pelted with stones, three times I was shipwrecked, I spent a night and a day in the open sea.

START The heart of Christianity is admitting you need help. Jesus said this about his true followers: "Healthy people don't need a doctor—sick people do. I have come to call not those who think they are righteous, but those who know they are sinners and need to repent" (Luke 5:31-32, NLT). But that honest humility doesn't mean Christians are weak. Just look, for example, at the endurance of the apostle Paul overviewed in this passage. The "they" he speaks of at the start are a group of people who claim to be spiritually superior to Paul. As he blasts back at their criticism, he proves just how tough Christians can be.

So what do you think—are Christians a herd of wimps?

READ 2 Corinthians 11:23-29

[23] Are they servants of Christ? (I am out of my mind to talk like this.) I am more. I have worked much harder, been in prison more frequently, been flogged more severely, and been exposed to death again and again. [24] Five times I received from the Jews the forty lashes minus one. [25] Three times I was beaten with rods, once I was pelted with stones, three times I was shipwrecked, I spent a night and a day in the open sea, [26] I have been constantly on the move. I have been in danger from rivers, in danger from bandits, in danger from my own people, in danger from Gentiles; in danger in the city, in danger in the country, in danger at sea; and in danger from false believers. [27] I have labored and toiled and have often gone without sleep; I have known hunger and thirst and have often gone without food; I have been cold and naked. [28] Besides everything else, I face daily the pressure of my concern for all the churches. [29] Who is weak, and I do not feel weak? Who is led into sin, and I do not inwardly burn?

THINK Next time you hear someone moan that Christians are hyper-cautious daddy's girls and mama's boys, ponder Paul's life. Jot a list of the hardships and suffering he's been through.

Paul faced terrible outward strains. What emotional or psychological pains did he endure?

What did Paul mean by the pressure he felt for "all the churches"?

God gave Paul the responsibility of spreading the good news about Jesus and overseeing the health of young, volatile churches set among hostile cultures. Acts 20:18-21 and 28-31 detail some of the weight he carried.

LIVE Does Paul's individual toughness prove anything about the strength of all Christians? Why—or why not?

If you had been stoned to death for your faith, no one would call you weak. Since you're presumably alive and well, how can you prove your faith doesn't make you a wimp?

Agree or disagree: People who go along with the crowd and give in to sin are the real pushovers.

WRAP Jesus said it straight: Going God's way is the toughest choice you can make. "'You can enter God's Kingdom only through the narrow gate,' he said. 'The highway to hell is broad, and its gate is wide for the many who choose the easy way. But the gateway to life is very narrow and the road is difficult, and only a few ever find it'" (Matthew 7:13-14, NLT).

》 MORE THOUGHTS TO MULL

- How does being a Christian help or hurt you in striving to play a tough but fair ball game, cutting a deal in the business world, or taking on any other challenge in life?

- When have you suffered for being a Christian yet hung tough?

- Read Matthew 5:44. Then pray for someone who roughs you up for following Jesus.

» MORE SCRIPTURES TO DIG

▪ Paul isn't the only believer to have suffered for his faith. Check this list from the book of Hebrews: "Others were tortured, refusing to turn from God in order to be set free. They placed their hope in a better life after the resurrection. Some were jeered at, and their backs were cut open with whips. Others were chained in prisons. Some died by stoning, and some were sawed in half, and others were killed with the sword. Some went about wearing skins of sheep and goats, destitute and oppressed and mistreated. They were too good for this world, wandering over deserts and mountains, hiding in caves and holes in the ground" (**Hebrews 11:35-38**, NLT).

▪ Sooner or later suffering becomes a part of every Christian's faith. Maybe it's the pain of persecution or maybe the sting of staying obedient. Paul once wrote, "For you have been given not only the privilege of trusting in Christ but also the privilege of suffering for him" (**Philippians 1:29**, NLT).

▪ Read Peter's encouragement to Christians who suffer in **1 Peter 1:3-9; 4:12-19**.

14. DEAD BONES

Matthew 23:27-28 (NLT)

Hypocrites! For you are like whitewashed tombs—beautiful on the outside but filled on the inside with dead people's bones and all sorts of impurity. Outwardly you look like righteous people, but inwardly your hearts are filled with hypocrisy and lawlessness.

START Plenty of people picture Jesus as meek and weak. But that isn't the Jesus of the Bible. He didn't always turn his cheek, and he didn't always let himself suffer violence at the hands of evil people. At choice moments he dished it out like no other. Look hard at his target—the Pharisees—the religious show-offs of Bible times. His words are like a top-ten list of things he hates about hypocrites.

What is a hypocrite? How do hypocrites affect your faith?

READ Matthew 23:1-7, 13, 27-28 (NLT)

[1] Then Jesus said to the crowds and to his disciples, [2] "The teachers of religious law and the Pharisees are the official interpreters of the law of Moses. [3] So practice and obey whatever they tell you, but don't follow their example. For they don't practice what they teach. [4] They crush people with unbearable religious demands and never lift a finger to ease the burden.

[5] "Everything they do is for show. On their arms they wear extra wide prayer boxes with Scripture verses inside, and they wear robes with extra long tassels. [6] And they love to sit at the head table at banquets and in the seats of honor in the synagogues. [7] They love to receive respectful greetings as they walk in the marketplaces, and to be called 'Rabbi.'

[13] "What sorrow awaits you teachers of religious law and you Pharisees. Hypocrites! For you shut the door of the Kingdom of Heaven in people's faces. You won't go in yourselves, and you don't let others enter either.

[27] "What sorrow awaits you teachers of religious law and you Pharisees. Hypocrites! For you are like whitewashed tombs—beautiful on the outside but filled on the inside with dead people's bones and all sorts of impurity. [28] Outwardly you look like righteous people, but inwardly your hearts are filled with hypocrisy and lawlessness.

THINK The Pharisees don't practice what they preach. What do they do instead?

Hypocrite literally means "mask," as in the masks Greek actors wore to pretend to be something they weren't. A hypocrite isn't a sincere but imperfect person but rather a persistent, religious fake, someone who claims to live close to God but doesn't.

The Pharisees accessorized their clothing with prayer boxes and long tassels, both symbols of their spirituality. The synagogue was a local center of worship, and *rabbi* meant "my master" or "my teacher." Why do the Pharisees do what they do?

Jesus says hypocrites "shut the door of the Kingdom of Heaven in people's faces." What does that mean?

How do Pharisees resemble "whitewashed tombs"?

LIVE When have you acted like a hypocrite—being a fake in your faith or in some other area of life?

When has the hypocrisy of others made you hesitant to follow Jesus or admit that you're a Christian?

How should God dispense with hypocrites?

Before you take it upon yourself to school your most-disliked hypocrite, know that God dislikes us pointing fingers at others when we have the same problem. "Examine yourselves," says 2 Corinthians 13:5, "to see if your faith is genuine" (NLT).

WRAP God is far more angry about hypocrites than any human can ever be. Jesus ends his speech with a warning: "You snakes! You brood of vipers! How will you escape being condemned to hell?" (Matthew 23:33).

>> MORE THOUGHTS TO MULL

- What does a non-hypocritical follower of Jesus look like? How can you avoid being a spiritual fake?

- Should God get the blame for hypocrites' nasty attitudes and actions? Why—or why not?

- If you can recall instances when you've acted hypocritically, get that straight with God. Then seek out the humans you hurt and get started on relationship repair.

>> MORE SCRIPTURES TO DIG

- Learn more about what hypocrisy looks like in **Isaiah 29:13-14**. Find out why God doesn't punish fakes right away in **Matthew 13:24-30, 36-43**. And check **James 4:7-10** and **Matthew 7:3-5** for instructions on how hypocrites can get right with God.

- Read all of **Matthew 23** to feel the heat of Jesus' judgment of hypocrites. But don't overlook his compassion even for these imposters. His speech closes with this cry: "Jerusalem, Jerusalem, you who kill the prophets and stone those sent to you, how often I have longed to gather your children together, as a hen gathers her chicks under her wings, and you were not willing" (**Matthew 23:37**).

15. SPEAK UP

1 Peter 3:15

Always be prepared to give an answer to everyone who asks you to give the reason for the hope that you have. But do this with gentleness and respect.

START Maybe some Christians talk about their faith only because they're supposed to, as an act of obedience to Jesus' command to "Go and make followers of all people in the world" (Matthew 28:19, NCV). But speaking up about Jesus is way more than a must-do. Jesus compared finding God to discovering a wildly expensive pearl, a prize worth giving your whole life to get (Matthew 13:45-46). The good news about Jesus is a treasure too big to keep to yourself.

Do you find it hard to speak up about Jesus? What makes it tough?

READ 1 Peter 3:15-18

15 But in your hearts revere Christ as the Lord. Always be prepared to give an answer to everyone who asks you to give the reason for the hope that you have. But do this with gentleness and respect, 16 keeping a clear conscience, so that those who speak maliciously against your behavior in Christ may be ashamed of their slander. 17 It is better, if it is God's will, to suffer for doing good than for doing evil. 18 For Christ also suffered once for sins, the righteous for the unrighteous, to bring you to God. He was put to death in the body but made alive in the Spirit.

THINK Not many people come to Christians with pointed questions like "What must I do to be saved?" (Acts 16:30). Their wonderings usually come in other words, like "Why are you different from everyone else?" or "Why do you go to church?" Their sharing a struggle can signal they want you to speak up about Jesus. So answer these: When you respond to people who wonder about your faith...

- What's your first task before you ever open your mouth?

- What should you be ready for?

- How should you speak?

What good is a clear conscience when you discuss spiritual issues with others?

What if you share respectfully, wisely, and without hypocrisy yet still get grief? How can you keep cool?

LIVE How would you want someone to talk to you about God?

Why don't Christians just keep quiet and let other people believe whatever they want?

How would you respond to someone who claims Christians always shove their beliefs down people's throats?

WRAP Being friends with God is too good to keep to yourself. It affects your attitudes. It moves out into your actions. And then it splashes over to other people. Whether you're just getting started with God or you've been a Christian a long time, don't hide what you have. There's a world waiting for it.

» MORE THOUGHTS TO MULL

- Think of someone you think might be surprised by this command to share "with gentleness and respect." Explain what it says, then ask what he or she thinks.

- Does this passage mean you should wait for people to ask you questions about your faith before you speak up?

- Describe your most positive experience of someone explaining Jesus to you.

» MORE SCRIPTURES TO DIG

- Check out **Acts 6:8-8:2**, where you'll catch Stephen calmly explaining God's good news to a hostile mob.

- Jesus always made sharing faith sound normal. Natural. Not nasty. Look at these two key teachings: In **Matthew 28:19-20**, Jesus said what we should do: "Therefore go and make disciples of all nations, baptizing them in the name of the Father and of the Son and of the Holy Spirit, and teaching them to obey everything I have commanded you. And surely I am with you always, to the very end of the age." That's called the Great Commission. And in **Acts 1:8** he made a Great Prediction about *how* and *where* we will do that: "But you will receive power when the Holy Spirit comes on you; and you will be my witnesses in Jerusalem, and in all Judea and Samaria, and to the ends of the earth."

- Look again at **Colossians 1:21-23** for a tight way to explain what Jesus has done for you. You'll find an easy to understand version at the end of study 7.

16. ASK AND RECEIVE

Why doesn't God answer all my prayers?

Luke 11:9-10

So I say to you: Ask and it will be given to you; seek and you will find; knock and the door will be opened to you. For everyone who asks receives; those who seek find; and to those who knock, the door will be opened.

START Jesus said to pray for what you want, pledging that his Father will always answer (Mark 11:24). The Bible even teaches that sometimes the reason you don't have what you want is because you haven't asked God for it (James 4:2). Those sound like foolproof, no-exception guarantees that God stands ready to dish up your every wish. So what's going on when you pray yet come up empty-handed?

What do you expect to happen when you pray?

READ Luke 11:5-13

> [5] Then Jesus said to them, "Suppose you have a friend, and you go to him at midnight and say, 'Friend, lend me three loaves of bread; [6] a friend of mine on a journey has come to me, and I have nothing to set before him.' [7] And suppose the one inside answers, 'Don't bother me. The door is already locked, and my children and I are in bed. I can't get up and give you anything.' [8] I tell you, even though he will not get up and give you the bread because of friendship, yet because of your shameless audacity he will surely get up and give you as much as you need. [9] So I say to you: Ask and it will be given to you; seek and you will find; knock and the door will be opened to you. [10] For everyone who asks receives; those who seek find; and to those who knock, the door will be opened. [11] Which of you fathers, if your son asks for a fish, will give him a snake instead? [12] Or if he asks for an egg, will give him a scorpion? [13] If you then, though you are evil, know how to give good gifts to your children, how much more will your Father in heaven give the Holy Spirit to those who ask him!"

THINK Why does that dazed friend in the parable finally get up and give in?

What does that say about God? How should we make requests to him?

Jesus just finished teaching his followers the words we know as the Lord's Prayer (Luke 11:1-4), where he leaves no doubt that God gives gladly. So his goal isn't to imply that God is some grouch who won't give us anything until we pester him mercilessly. The parable says more about the attitude God wants from us. God's main goal is to build in us a persistent trust that keeps asking and continues believing in God's total goodness.

What one thing does God promise to always give us if we ask?

We might hanker for Jet Skis, Ferraris, and Moto Guzzis. But the gift God gives without exception is himself.

LIVE When have you prayed and gotten an obvious "yes!" from God? When have you heard him say "no"? Has he ever answered, "not now"?

Suppose you pray and don't get what you want. Has God ignored your request—or not? Explain.

If God's goal is to teach you to trust that he always desires what's best for you, then how should you react when your wants go unmet?

First John 5:14-15 says you can be confident about getting your request under one crucial condition—that you ask according to God's will. Big meaning: Ask for what you believe to be good, but let God answer in his time, in his way.

WRAP God doesn't roll over, pull the covers over his head, and pack his ears with pillow fluff. He has more wisdom than you can fathom. He's too good to give in to every whim or wish. So trust God even when you don't understand his answers.

» MORE THOUGHTS TO MULL

- Ask some mature Christian friends how God has answered their prayers.

- How can you guarantee you will always get what you ask God for?

- How would you explain all this to a friend who feels stung because "God didn't answer my prayers"?

» MORE SCRIPTURES TO DIG

- Jesus makes the same point here that **James 1:17** makes toward the back of the Bible: God only knows how to give great gifts. James wrote, "Every good action and every perfect gift is from God. These good gifts come down from the Creator of the sun, moon, and stars, who does not change like their shifting shadows" (NCV).

- Prayer isn't just about asking. It's about applauding God (**Psalm 18:25-31**). It includes confessing what you've done wrong (**Psalm 51:1-5, 7, 10**). At times it demands silence (**Job 40:1-9**). And it concludes with yielding, telling God you want exactly what he wants for you (**Matthew 26:36-46**).

- Look at **Matthew 18:19-20** to spot the importance of praying with other people. And study **Luke 18:10-14** and **Matthew 5:22-24** to see some bad Bible prayers.

17. WISE ONES

Does God want to wreck my life?

Matthew 7:24

Therefore everyone who hears these words of mine and puts them into practice is like a wise man who built his house on the rock.

START Jesus was known for his pithy wisdom and parables. But in the Sermon on the Mount, he breaks out a lengthy description of God's wisdom for life. In Matthew, he starts with the Beatitudes, explains how to get truly happy (5:1-12). Then he details God's commands for standing out from the world (5:13-16), handling anger (5:21-26), sex (5:27-32), dealing with enemies (5:38-48), prayer (6:5-15 and 7:7-12), not stuffing yourself with stuff (6:25-34), and judging (7:1-5). But if you're worried that Jesus lays down the law just to make a mess of your fun, check out what he says in the last words of his message.

Why do you suppose God makes rules?

READ Matthew 7:24-27

> [24] "Therefore everyone who hears these words of mine and puts them into practice is like a wise man who built his house on the rock. [25] The rain came down, the streams rose, and the winds blew and beat against that house; yet it did not fall, because it had its foundation on the rock. [26] But everyone who hears these words of mine and does not put them into practice is like a foolish man who built his house on sand. [27] The rain came down, the streams rose, and the winds blew and beat against that house, and it fell with a great crash."

THINK What does Jesus call the guy or gal who follows his instructions for life? What good will it do to obey Jesus?

Where does the second guy go wrong? How does that turn out?

Why were the crowds awed by Jesus' teaching? What does that mean?

The other religious leaders of Jesus' day passed on secondhand spiritual information. Jesus defined and lived the truth he preached.

LIVE Let's assume the guy who built his house on the beach was enjoying a heap of fun until the rain came along and wiped out his sandcastle. So is he really the stupid one—or not? Why?

How is it possible to hear God's words and not put them into practice? Describe what that looks like.

What's the right-here-right-now payoff for putting God's words into practice?

Get honest: Are you building your life on rock—or sand? Explain.

WRAP Nothing God forbids is fun in the long run for all people affected. The Lord is totally mighty, caring, and smart. Ponder it: He's Ultimate Power, so he could force you to obey his commands. But he's also Ultimate Love and Ultimate Intelligence. That makes him worth obeying with your whole life. That thing we think will make us ecstatic might really be more like slamming a hand in a car door.

» MORE THOUGHTS TO MULL

- Make a list of bad things you've thought about trying. Then add to your list God's good reasons not to.

- Would you guess that most people in your world are wise—or foolish? Based on what evidence?

- Are you glad God spells out right and wrong for your life? Why—or why not?

» MORE SCRIPTURES TO DIG

▪ Anyone with one eyeball can see that bad people often win in this world. And you might wonder if evildoers will always get away with wickedness. People in the Bible puzzled over that too—until they saw what God has planned. Check this Old Testament Bible explanation: "Then I went into your sanctuary, O God, and I finally understood the destiny of the wicked. Truly, you put them on a slippery path and send them sliding over the cliff to destruction. In an instant they are destroyed, completely swept away by terrors. When you arise, O Lord, you will laugh at their silly ideas as a person laughs at dreams in the morning" (**Psalm 73:17-20**, NLT).

▪ **John 14:23** says that when you choose to obey God's rules, you get tight with God. Check out Jesus' words: "All who love me will do what I say. My Father will love them, and we will come to and make our home with each of them" (NLT).

18. HIDE AND SEEK

Is God out to get me?

Psalm 103:11

For as high as the heavens are above the earth, so great is his love for those who fear him.

START Some people picture God as a furious deity who wants to rip us limb from limb for sin. And yes, it's true that God is the "righteous Judge" (2 Timothy 4:8), the one Jesus said can "destroy both soul and body in hell" (Matthew 10:28). But God wants to be friends with anyone who allows him in (Revelation 3:20), and his greatest goal is for the whole world to know him (2 Peter 3:9). Check out the fresh picture of God that David offers in this Old Testament song.

Do you ever worry that God wants to hunt you down and hurt you?

READ Psalm 103:1-14

> [1] Praise the Lord, my soul; all my inmost being, praise his holy name.

> [2] Praise the Lord, my soul, and forget not all his benefits—

> [3] who forgives all your sins and heals all your diseases,

> [4] who redeems your life from the pit and crowns you with love and compassion,

> [5] who satisfies your desires with good things so that your youth is renewed like the eagle's.

> [6] The Lord works righteousness and justice for all the oppressed.

> [7] He made known his ways to Moses, his deeds to the people of Israel:

> [8] The Lord is compassionate and gracious, slow to anger, abounding in love.

> [9] He will not always accuse, nor will he harbor his anger forever;

¹⁰ he does not treat us as our sins deserve or repay us according to our iniquities.

¹¹ For as high as the heavens are above the earth, so great is his love for those who fear him;

¹² as far as the east is from the west, so far has he removed our transgressions from us.

¹³ As a father has compassion on his children, so the Lord has compassion on those who fear him;

¹⁴ for he knows how we are formed, he remembers that we are dust.

THINK Right away David launches into praise God for "all his benefits." Name at least half a dozen good things God does.

What motivates God to do all this?

Do people get what their sins deserve? Why not?

What does God do with our sin?

God does better than cut us slack. He gets rid of our sins completely. In Isaiah 43:25 God says "I—yes, I alone—will blot out your sins for my own sake and will never think of them again" (NLT).

LIVE Why does God have compassion on us?

Should you be scared of God? Why—or why not?

WRAP God is far more eager to help you than to hurt you. Like Psalm 103:17 says, "The LORD's love for those who respect him continues forever and ever" (NCV).

» MORE THOUGHTS TO MULL

- If you've never told God you need and want his forgiveness, tell him now.

- Have you ever done something bad and wondered if God would still love you? How did you deal with that?

- How would you feel about a God who never judges evil? How about one who doesn't figure out a just way to forgive us?

» MORE SCRIPTURES TO DIG

- In **Acts 13:22** God called David "a man after my own heart." Yet if you read **Psalm 51**, you discover David had major sins to straighten out with God. The point? You can trust David's firsthand information on God's forgiveness.

- Study **Psalm 19:12-14** to see how David invites God to help him spot his own sins.

- Whether you're getting to know God for the first time or want to keep your relationship with him fresh, God wants you to admit your wrongs to him. As **1 John 1:8-9** explains, "If we say we have no sin, we are fooling ourselves, and the truth is not in us. But if we confess our sins, he will forgive our sins, because we can trust God to do what is right. He will cleanse us from all the wrongs we have done" (NCV). Jesus died for all people (**1 John 2:2**), but his death doesn't do us any good if we don't ask for and accept his forgiveness.

19. SPIDER FIRE

Is hell real?

Revelation 20:15

All whose names were not found written in the book of life were thrown into the lake of fire.

START On July 8, 1741, New England pastor Jonathan Edwards preached his infamous sermon "Sinners in the Hands of an Angry God," rattling off phrases like this: "The God that holds you over the pit of hell, much as one holds a spider, or some loathsome insect over the fire, abhors you, and is dreadfully provoked; his wrath toward you burns like fire; he looks upon you as worthy of nothing else, but to be cast into the fire." God is indeed the righteous judge of the universe. But lots of people think Edwards makes him sound eager to toss sinners on a cosmic barbeque. How can a good God cook up such a fiery place?

Do you think the idea of hell wrecks God's reputation? Why—or why not?

READ Revelation 20:7-15

[7] When the thousand years are over, Satan will be released from his prison [8] and will go out to deceive the nations in the four corners of the earth—Gog and Magog—and to gather them for battle. In number they are like the sand on the seashore. [9] They marched across the breadth of the earth and surrounded the camp of God's people, the city he loves. But fire came down from heaven and devoured them. [10] And the devil, who deceived them, was thrown into the lake of burning sulfur, where the beast and the false prophet had been thrown. They will be tormented day and night for ever and ever.

[11] Then I saw a great white throne and him who was seated on it. The earth and the heavens fled from his presence, and there was no place for them. [12] And I saw the dead, great and small, standing before the throne, and books were opened. Another book was opened, which is the book of life. The dead were judged according to what they had done as recorded in the books. [13] The sea gave up

the dead that were in it, and death and Hades gave up the dead that were in them, and everyone was judged according to what they had done. [14] Then death and Hades were thrown into the lake of fire. The lake of fire is the second death. [15] All whose names were not found written in the book of life were thrown into the lake of fire.

THINK What does the Devil do wrong? What's his punishment?

The Beast and the False Prophet—two evil characters from earlier in Revelation—were tossed into the burning sulfur back in Revelation 19:20. The idea of the Devil and his crew getting toasted isn't objectionable to most people. But who faces God's judgment next?

"The earth and the heavens fled from his presence" is a poetic way of saying that, when compared to God's majesty, everything else fades to insignificance.

Who gets spared from the lake of fire?

That "book of life" is a concrete way of saying "the people who belong to God" (Revelation 13:8; 17:8; 21:27). Some Bible scholars argue that this scene doesn't involve the people whose names appear in the book of life, since Christians "have already passed from death into life" (John 5:24, NLT).

LIVE Do you think hell is a good idea? Explain.

While hell sounds harsh, it's actually a confirmation of our freedom to choose how we live. Hell shows the evilness of evil. It displays the rightness of God. It fulfills justice. And it helps us know evil really does get punished.

Why do people end up in hell?

Hell gives its occupants an eternity of what they've chosen in this life: An existence without God. Like Billy Graham has said, "God will never send anybody to hell. If man goes to hell, he goes by his own free choice." Medieval Italian poet Dante Alighieri (1265-1321) wrote that "If you insist on having your own way, you will get it. Hell is the enjoyment of your own way forever."

WRAP Hell is ultimately a choice, because God offers people a way out of judgment. Romans 6:23 says, "For the wages of sin is death, but the gift of God is eternal life in Christ Jesus our Lord." You can tell God you know Jesus died in your place. You can thank him for providing forgiveness for you. And when you start your new life with God, being close to him lasts forever.

»   MORE THOUGHTS TO MULL

- Do you believe hell is a real place? Why—or why not? Is it an actual lake of fire or something else?

- How would you explain hell to someone who doesn't buy the Bible?

- What would the universe be like if there were no hell?

»   MORE SCRIPTURES TO DIG

- See what Jesus has to say about hell in **Matthew 10:28**.

- The Bible calls hell an "unquenchable fire" (**Matthew 3:12**), "damnation" (**Matthew 23:33, KJV**), a "furnace of fire" (**Matthew 13:42, 50, KJV**), "blackest darkness" (**Jude 13**), and here, "a fiery lake of burning sulfur" (**Revelation 21:8**).

- To fully grasp the awfulness of hell, study its opposite. Catch a glimpse of heaven in **Revelation 4, 21, and 22**. You'll look at a section of Revelation 21 in the next study.

20. TO VALHALLA—OR NOT

What is heaven like?

Revelation 21:3-4

"Look! God's dwelling place is now among the people, and he will dwell with them. They will be his people, and God himself will be with them and be their God. 'He will wipe every tear from their eyes. There will be no more death' or mourning or crying or pain."

START If you'd been a good Viking warrior in the days of old, you would have longed to die and head to Valhalla, the hall of slain heroes. In Valhalla, hearty men battle by day and banquet by night with Odin, king of the gods. Warriors are served by the Valkyries, a band of warrior-maidens. If you aren't chosen for Valhalla, however, you wind up in a dim, underground world run by a goddess named Hel, daughter of Loki, the spirit of evil. But maybe that's not what you had in mind for your forever.

People in every time and place have told tales of life after death. The Bible claims you have a room booked in heaven for all eternity. So what do you expect heaven to be like?

READ Revelation 21:1-7

> [1] Then I saw "a new heaven and a new earth," for the first heaven and the first earth had passed away, and there was no longer any sea. [2] I saw the Holy City, the new Jerusalem, coming down out of heaven from God, prepared as a bride beautifully dressed for her husband. [3] And I heard a loud voice from the throne saying, "Look! God's dwelling place is now among the people, and he will dwell with them. They will be his people, and God himself will be with them and be their God. [4] 'He will wipe every tear from their eyes. There will be no more death' or mourning or crying or pain, for the old order of things has passed away."
>
> [5] He who was seated on the throne said, "I am making everything new!" Then he said, "Write this down, for these words are trustworthy and true."
>
> [6] He said to me: "It is done. I am the Alpha and the Omega, the Beginning and the End. To the thirsty I will give water without cost from the spring of the water of life. [7] Those who are victorious will inherit all this, and I will be their God and they will be my children.

THINK What drops out of the sky at the start of this scene? What happened to all the old stuff?

If you're at all attached to earth you might read that verse and feel like mom cleaned house and tossed out your Barbies or baseball cards. But new doesn't mean God trashed the old, but rather that he remade it. "No sea" means God has gotten rid of chaos.

That "Holy City" is a place. But "bride" indicates it's also a group of people—God's people, as perfect as a decked-out bride. Sounds confusing, yet the image captures two concepts.

Picturing what the Holy City looks like is exciting. But there's bigger news: Who will live there?

What happened to pain, crying, and everything bad?

This new heaven and earth embodies the perfection God planned for us in the first place. It's the "very good" world you read about back in Genesis. And it's a party open to all. Revelation 22:17 says "Let those who are thirsty come; and let all who wish take the free gift of the water of life."

LIVE Does this description of heaven live up to your expectations? Why—or why not?

Whatever we've enjoyed of God's creation—music, nature, color, beauty— will be given to us in abundance, with boggling intensity. Revelation 21:9-27 describes gold streets, along with emeralds, amethyst, and pearls. Harps show up in Revelation 5:8, but it doesn't look like everyone gets one. Because our dreams right now can be limited and warped, we're in for incredible surprises.

If heaven is full of amazing stuff, what do you think will grab your attention when you get there?

WRAP Whatever heaven is like, focusing on the stuff of heaven is like going to a Hollywood bash and looking no further than the appetizers. God is the real hit of this party. The most sensational thing about heaven isn't the where or the what. It's the who. You'll hang out with God and his friends forever.

» MORE THOUGHTS TO MULL

- What about heaven makes it sound like a great place?

- What painful things do you look forward to God wiping away in heaven?

- What can you do right now to bring a slice of heaven to earth? How is that possible?

» MORE SCRIPTURES TO DIG

- The theme of God living close to his people runs all through Scripture. God is preparing a people to live with him for eternity in heaven. Check out these God-is-building-a-people verses: **Genesis 17:7, Exodus 6:7, Leviticus 26:12, Jeremiah 31:33, Ezekiel 11:20, 2 Corinthians 6:16, Hebrews 8:10,** and **1 Peter 2:9-10.**

- Back in the Old Testament the idea of life after death was hazy. Only in the New Testament does it become clear that when God talked about hanging out with his people, he meant forever, post-death. Here's what's happening in heaven: God's will is done fully (**Matthew 6:10**). Our bodies will be changed (**2 Corinthians 5:1-5**). And there's rocking worship (**Revelation 4**).

- Heaven is more than a hope. It's a promise for people who believe in Jesus (**John 14:1-3**). Whether you know it or not, it's your real home (**Philippians 3:20**). If you know Jesus, you have accommodations booked there for all eternity (**John 3:16**).

Designed for middle schoolers, the Deeper Bible studies provide you with a unique and effective tool for your students. Use in large or small groups to help communicate God's truth in a way that connects with young teens and shows them what faith can look like in their everyday lives.

Choose
Steer Wide of Total Stupidity
978-0-310-27493-3

Stick
Glue Yourself to Godly Friends
978-0-310-27490-2

Pray
Talk to the King of the Universe
978-0-310-27492-6

Trust
Meet the World's One Savior and Lord
978-0-310-27489-6

Kevin Johnson
Retail $7.99 each

Visit www.youthspecialties.com
or your local bookstore

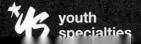

youth
specialties

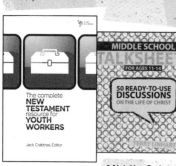